OHS form 1

CODE
EXIT

GW01044220

My Mars Trip

Jillian Powell

Contents

OXFORD
UNIVERSITY PRESS

Mini, Macro and Micro World!

Hello. My name is **Mini Marvel**. My dad **Macro Marvel** and I invented **Micro World**. This is the book that inspired us to make the **Galactic Orbit** zone.

My dad Macro Marvel

You are here

Did you know?

This is a glossary. It tells you the meaning of some of the words in the text.

Glossary

cams	tools for getting snaps
scoop	to pick up
secure	will not fall off
soil	mix of dust and bits of rock

Fact!

The largest volcano in the solar system is on Mars. It is called Olympus Mons.

Mini's Top Spot

Can you find the contents page?

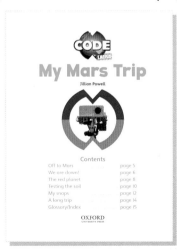

My Mars Trip

Jillian Powell

Contents

OXFORD
UNIVERSITY PRESS

Before you read

Sound checker
Say the sounds.

ow   oi   air
ear   ure

Tricky words

be	are	me
they	we	he
all	was	she
my	you	her

Sound spotter
Blend the sounds.

p	ow	er

j	oi	n

y	ear	s

p	air	s

s	e	c	ure

Into the zone
Humans have not been to Mars but space scientists have sent robots to explore the red planet.

4

Off to Mars

I am a Mars bot.
Soon I will be on my way to Mars.
They check all my parts are **secure**.

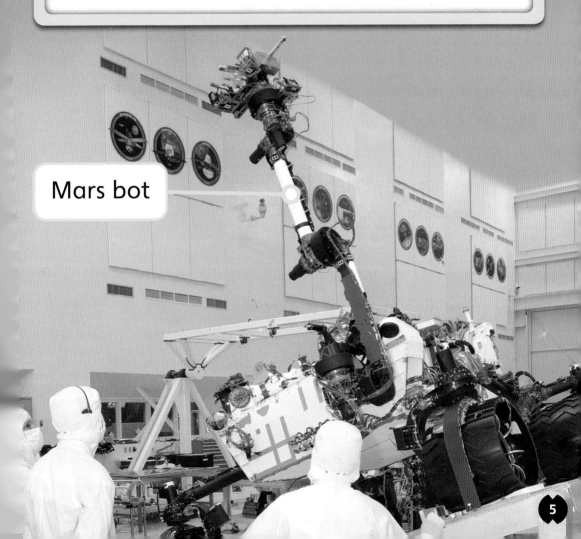

Mars bot

We are down!

It was a long ride!
Now you can join me on
the red planet.

The red planet

A lot of the rocks are red on this planet.

I test the air.

It is not pure.

No trees grow on Mars.

Testing the soil

I test what is in the **soil**.
My hand opens out to
scoop it up.

My snaps

I see a crack in a rock.

Is it a door?

I get near and snap it.

lots of pairs
of **cams**

A long trip

I will be on Mars for years.

You can **track** me across Mars!

He will track me too.

She can see me on her screen.

Glossary

cams	tools for getting snaps
scoop	to pick up
secure	will not fall off
soil	mix of dust and bits of rock
track	to go after

Index

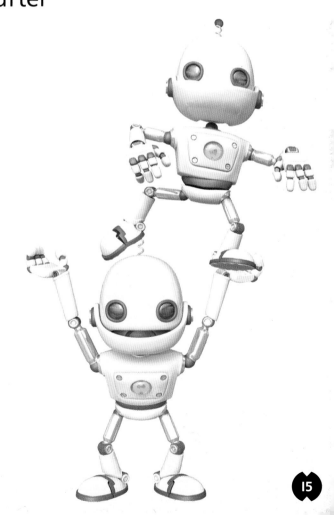

Now you have read ...
My Mars Trip

Text checker

What does the Mars bot do? Decide whether
these statements are true or false:

It plants trees.	True	False
It tests the soil.	True	False
It takes pictures of the planet.	True	False
It talks to aliens.	True	False

MITE fun

Have another look at the picture on page 14.
Where do you think this place is?
What sort of work are the people doing?